Fascinating INSECTS

Dragonflies

Aaron Carr

LET'S READ AV2 BY WEIGL

ADDED VALUE • AUDIO VISUAL

Go to www.av2books.com, and enter this book's unique code.

BOOK CODE

N683740

AV2 by Weigl brings you media enhanced books that support active learning.

AV2 provides enriched content that supplements and complements this book. Weigl's AV2 books strive to create inspired learning and engage young minds in a total learning experience.

Your AV2 Media Enhanced books come alive with...

Audio
Listen to sections of the book read aloud.

Video
Watch informative video clips.

Embedded Weblinks
Gain additional information for research.

Try This!
Complete activities and hands-on experiments.

Key Words
Study vocabulary, and complete a matching word activity.

Quizzes
Test your knowledge.

Slide Show
View images and captions, and prepare a presentation.

...and much, much more!

Published by AV2 by Weigl
350 5th Avenue, 59th Floor New York, NY 10118
Website: www.av2books.com   www.weigl.com

Library of Congress Control Number: 2013939650
ISBN 978-1-62127-964-8 (hardcover)
ISBN 978-1-62127-966-2 (softcover)

Printed in the United States of America in North Mankato, Minnesota
1 2 3 4 5 6 7 8 9 0 17 16 15 14 13

052013
WEP040413

Project Coordinator: Aaron Carr   Art Director: Terry Paulhus

Weigl acknowledges Getty Images as the primary image supplier for this title.

Dragonflies

CONTENTS

3

Meet the dragonfly.

Dragonflies are insects.
They have long, colorful bodies.

Dragonflies can be found all around the world.

All around the world, dragonflies live near water.

Dragonflies are born
when they hatch from eggs.

When they hatch from eggs, dragonflies live under water.

Dragonflies live most of their lives under water.

Under water, dragonflies eat and grow until they are ready to live on land.

Dragonflies have two pairs of large wings.

Two pairs of large wings
help dragonflies move around.

Dragonflies can not fly
when they are cold.

When they are cold, they sit in sunlight until they get warm.

Dragonflies have very large eyes.

With very large eyes, dragonflies
can see in almost all directions at once.

Dragonflies eat small insects.

Eating small insects gives dragonflies everything they need to be healthy.

Dragonflies are important in nature.

In nature, dragonflies help keep the number of pests down.

DRAGONFLY FACTS

These pages provide more detail about the interesting facts found in the book. They are intended to be used by adults as a learning support to help young readers round out their knowledge of each insect or arachnid featured in the *Fascinating Insects* series.

Pages 4–5

Dragonflies are insects. Insects are small animals with segmented bodies and six jointed legs. They have hard shells, called exoskeletons, with three parts: the head, the thorax, and the abdomen. There are more than 5,000 species of dragonfly. Dragonflies have long, thin bodies that can be up to 6 inches (15 centimeters) long. Their bodies have very bright coloring. Dragonflies can be blue, green, red, yellow, orange, or brown.

Pages 6–7

Dragonflies can be found all around the world. They live on every continent except Antarctica. Dragonflies are most often found near bodies of fresh water, such as lakes, ponds, and rivers. Dragonflies lay their eggs near slow-moving freshwater sources, including swamps and bogs. Some species lay eggs in water. Other species lay eggs in mud near water, while still others lay eggs on aquatic plants.

Pages 8–9

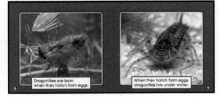

Dragonflies are born when they hatch from eggs. Dragonfly larvae live in water after hatching. Young dragonflies are called nymphs. They molt, or shed their skin, several times as they grow. Nymphs breathe through gills and eat insects, tadpoles, and small fish. When they leave the water, nymphs molt one last time. During this molt, the long body and wings emerge. After this, the dragonfly is a fully grown adult.

Pages 10–11

Dragonflies live most of their lives underwater. Depending on the species, they may spend a few weeks or a few years living underwater as nymphs. The dragonfly nymph breathes through gills near its tail. The nymph breathes water into its body through these gills. In emergencies, it can push the water back out very quickly. The force of this action pushes the nymph forward through the water faster than it could swim otherwise.

Pages 12–13

Dragonflies have two pairs of large wings. The dragonfly's wings are usually see-through, but they have complex patterns of veins. Its wingspan can be up to 7 inches (18 cm) wide. When not flying, the dragonfly holds its wings out to the sides. Dragonflies are often mistaken for damselflies. However, the damselfly folds its wings back along the length of its body when it is not flying. Also, dragonfly wings are all the same size, while damselflies have two large wings and two smaller wings.

Pages 14–15

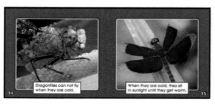

Dragonflies cannot fly when they are cold. They sit in sunlight until they warm up enough to fly. Sometimes, they flap their wings quickly to create heat. Once they are warm enough to fly, dragonflies are among the best fliers in the world. Some dragonflies can reach speeds up to 20 miles (30 kilometers) an hour. Dragonflies are also very agile. They can fly straight up or down, hover in place, turn quickly, and even fly backwards.

Pages 16–17

Dragonflies have very large eyes. The dragonfly has two compound eyes. These big eyes cover most of a dragonfly's head and are made up of as many as 30,000 lenses, called ommatidia. The dragonfly has excellent vision. It can see a wider range of colors than humans, and it can see in almost 360 degrees. Scientists believe dragonflies may use up to 80 percent of their brain to process visual information from their eyes.

Pages 18–19

Dragonflies eat small insects. As carnivores, dragonflies prey on smaller insects, such as mosquitoes, flies, and aphids. They rely on their speed and keen eyesight to capture prey. Dragonflies are the most efficient predators in the animal kingdom, successfully catching their prey on 95 percent of their attempts. They use their legs to catch prey, which can be more than half their own size. Dragonflies get most of the water they need from the food they eat.

Pages 20–21

Dragonflies are important in nature. As predators, dragonflies play an important role in the ecosystems in which they live. Dragonflies help control the populations of many insects that share their habitats. They are also food for larger predators, such as fish, ducks, and water shrews. Scientists regard dragonflies as indicator species. This means they study dragonflies to see if wetland or freshwater ecosystems are healthy.

KEY WORDS

Research has shown that as much as 65 percent of all written material published in English is made up of 300 words. These 300 words cannot be taught using pictures or learned by sounding them out. They must be recognized by sight. This book contains 48 common sight words to help young readers improve their reading fluency and comprehension. This book also teaches young readers several important content words. These words are paired with pictures to aid in learning and improve understanding.

Page	Sight Words First Appearance
4	the
5	are, have, long, they
6	all, around, be, can, found, live, near, water, world
8	from, when
9	under
10	most, of, their
11	and, eat, grow, land, on, to, until
12	large, two
13	help, move
14	not
15	get, in
16	almost, at, eyes, once, see, very, with
18	small
19	gives, need
20	down, important, keep, number

Page	Content Words First Appearance
4	dragonfly
5	bodies, insects
8	eggs
12	pairs, wings
15	sunlight
16	directions
18	insects
19	everything
20	nature, pests

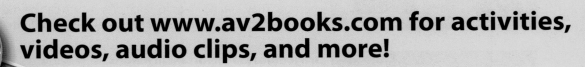